What is the Father's Plan?

Doug Roberts

What is the Father's Plan?
by Doug Roberts

Unless otherwise indicated, scripture quotations are taken from *The Message, The Bible in Contemporary Language*, Eugene Peterson, 2002, Used by Permission of NavPress, All Rights Reserved. www.navpress.com (1-800-366-7788).

ISBN: 978-0-9825992-8-0

I want to thank Ed Chinn, Fred White, Rob Hatch, Shellie Kushnerick and Rita Roberts for all there help in getting this to print.

Printed in the United States of America

Table of Contents

Chapter 1 — We Are the Focus of His Love

Do you realize the Father has a plan for you?

Some accept Jesus Christ as Lord and Savior but still hang onto the idea that they're just trying to escape from hell, just trying to make it to heaven. But, the Father's plan reaches so far beyond that. We need to know that He has a plan for us, and that He wants to accomplish it *in* us and *through* us and *for* us while we're here on the earth.

So it's one thing to know Jesus as your Lord and Savior - which is very important - but it's also crucial to know Jesus is the doorway to the Father. Through Him, the Father can make Himself known to us. He wants to come live and abide within us because we are His children. And He wants to use us to accomplish the things He called us to do.

In order to grasp this message, I want to lead you through the first chapter of Ephesians. I'm going to read verses 3 through 14 from *The Message*.

"How blessed is God and what a blessing he is. He is the Father of our master, Jesus Christ, and he takes us to high places of blessing in him." — vs. 3

Think of it; the Apostle Paul chooses to introduce the great God of the whole universe as the Father of our master Jesus Christ. Now Paul could have introduced God in any way He wanted. But He made it known that He is the Father. And, when we think of a father, what do we first think of? We think of a family; we think of children.

I think Paul introduced Him to us as the Father because He wants to be our Father and He wants us to be His children. And He wants to bless us as a father blesses his children. He is the Father of our master Jesus Christ and He takes us to high places of blessing in Jesus.

everything the Father has for us, is found in Jesus. Everything the Father wants to do through us is found in Jesus. Everything the Father wants to bless us with is found in Jesus.

Please understand that everything the Father has for us is found in Jesus. Everything the Father wants to do through us is found in Jesus. Everything the Father wants to bless us with is found in Jesus. Jesus tells us there's no way to the Father except through Himself; Jesus is the door.

It does not matter how good you are or how much you know; there is only one way to the Father, and that is through Jesus Christ (John 14:6). When you accept Jesus Christ as your Lord and Savior, then you have access to the Father. And the Father can then come and abide and live within you because then you become the dwelling place of the Father.

Let's move on:

"Long before he laid down earth's foundation, he had us in mind and he had settled on us as the focus of his love to be made whole and holy by his love." — vs. 4

Think about it; before God ever spoke the world into existence, before He ever created anything, He had us in mind, and He had settled on us to be the focus of His love.

Here's the Father, the God of all creation; He holds the universe in His hand. Before He ever spoke the world into existence, He was thinking of you. He had you in His mind. And His thoughts for you were how He could bless you and fulfill His destiny in you. And He wanted you to be the focus of His love on the earth.

Who is the focus of His love on the earth? You Are! That's what it says. He had you in mind and He had settled on you to be the focus of His love!

He had us in mind and He wanted us to be the focus of His love because He chose us and He appointed us. In John 15 Jesus said, "You didn't choose me, I chose you." God chose us in Christ to be the focus of His love, the ambassador of His kingdom. Everything He wants to do on the earth He will do through us His family. He has *limited Himself* to accomplishing His work in the way.

Why? Because that's His plan.

Chapter 2 — The Father Believes in Us

Let's continue in Ephesians 1, as told in *The Message*:

"Long, long ago he decided to adopt us into his family, through Jesus Christ. (What pleasure he took in planning this!) He wanted us to enter into the celebration of his lavish gift-giving by the hand of his beloved son."

— vs. 5 & 6

My goodness, this just gets better and better! He—the Father—decided to adopt us into his family. A father wants children. So He decided to adopt us into His family through Jesus Christ. And He took pleasure in planning all of this. He wanted us to enter into the celebration of His lavish gift-giving by the hand of His beloved Son.

God wants to love us extravagantly. He wants to lavish the gifts and the blessings He has for us. God's not a selfish god. God believes in us. *He is for us.*

> God said, "If you'll quit trying so hard and just rest in the fact that I am God and I am for you and not against you, it'll make your life a lot easier."

Years ago the Lord spoke to me, "I have more faith in you than you have in me." When I asked for more, He said, "If you'll quit trying so hard and just rest in the fact that I am God and I am for you and not against you, it'll make your life a lot easier."

And, what He said brought revelation. I suddenly saw, and I said to Him, "Okay, so Father, I have more faith in You and who You are than in me and my ability to hear You. Because you are God, the Father, and the Creator of all things. You designed and formed my body. So I have faith in Your ability to do whatever is needed to be done, for me to be able to walk in the things You called for me to do. So my faith says, "Yes!"

Now when God asks me to go places and do things, I say "Yes." When He confirms it by releasing the finances for it and opening doors to it, that is when I will walk boldly into those things. Therefore I am being sent, not just going on my own. It's one thing to go, but another thing to be sent. When the Father sends you out, then you have all Kingdom authority to do the works that He sent you there to do.

So, let your faith be "Yes," but wait for His sending, which includes finances. The Father has never asked you to finance His Kingdom. Don't go in debt trying to build His Kingdom.

When He adopted us, He changed our name. He is now our Father. We are His sons and daughters here on the earth. He also chose us to be ambassadors of His kingdom.

We are new creations, new creatures. We are no longer who we were. There was a time in my life when the devil was my father because I didn't know Jesus as my Lord and Savior. But I'm no longer obligated to serve the devil! I have a new Father now. My Father is God, the Creator of the universe. He is unlimited in His resources, His revelation, and His love. Because He is my Father now, I'm not limited by my old nature. Because I am walking as a new creation in Christ Jesus.

Let's go on Ephesians 1.

"Because of the sacrifice of the Messiah, his blood poured out on the altar of the cross, we are a free people. Free of penalties and punishments chalked up by our misdeeds. And not just barely free, Abundantly free." — vs. 7

When Jesus paid the price for our sin, it set us free from our sin. When Jesus hung on the cross and said, "It is finished," it was literally finished. He did everything that the Father required for our sins. So when we accept him as Lord and Savior, His blood cleanses us from all of our unrighteousness. We become holy, complete, and righteous in Christ now.

So when God sees me, He doesn't see who I *was*, He sees who I *am*. And who I am is now hidden in Christ. It is in Christ that we now live. It is in Christ now that we move and have our being (Acts 17:28).

It's not what I do, it's what Christ did. You can't earn salvation, it's a free gift. You can't earn God's love, He chose to love you. He decided to do that before you ever drew breath.

Chapter 3 — Who Am I?

When I was in the world, God loved me. I didn't know Him, but He loved me. When I accepted Jesus Christ as my Lord and Savior, God loved me. The only thing that changed was my relationship with Him. His love for me was the same when I was in the world as it is now that I'm a son.

It's my relationship. When I was in the world, I didn't know God as my Father. Now that I'm a son, I call him Father. I come boldly into His throne saying, "Good morning, Father!" I can do that because I'm his son. Not only am I His son, but I am His son. By His choice, not my own.

Do You understand? That is true, not according to *our* works, but according to Jesus (Gal 2:16)

The Bible says in 2 Corinthians 5:17, "Old things have passed away, new things have come." (NAS) You see, we are not who we were. He has made us alive in Christ. We are now the righteousness of God in Christ Jesus. We are holy. We are blameless. We are complete, lacking nothing."

That's what the Word of God says about us. That is who we are. So when you look at yourself in the mirror, don't listen to the lie of the enemy about who you were, because who you *were* is not who you *are*. You are now the righteousness of God in Christ. You are holy.

That's what the Word of God says about you. That's what the Father says about you. That's what Jesus says about you!

Let's return to Ephesians 1:

"He thought of everything, provided for everything we could possibly need, letting us in on the plans he took such delight in making. He set it all out before us in Christ, a long-range plan in which everything would be brought together and summed up in him, everything in the deepest heaven, everything on planet earth. It's in Christ that we find out who we are and what we are living for." — vs. 8-11

Think about this: God took delight in the plans he made for you in Christ Jesus. And

What He predestined us to be in Christ Jesus, has already been accomplished in Christ Jesus.

he thought of everything. There's nothing lacking in Christ. There's nothing incomplete. We're fully established. We have everything we need in order to be what God has created us to be in Christ Jesus. What He predestined us to be in Christ Jesus, has already been accomplished in Christ Jesus.

Every blessing the Father has for you, for me, and for us is found in Christ. That's why it's so essential for us to come into an understanding of our identity. We must clearly see who we are in Christ. When we understand who we are in Christ, the revelation of the kingdom of God opens up to a full understanding. It's not a mystery any longer because Jesus has chosen to make known the mystery to us.

Do you understand? The kingdom of God is not a mystery, once we know who we are in Christ and we come into an understanding of our authority as sons of God. That's because the kingdom of God is *in us*. Wherever we set our foot, there—right there in our footprint—is the kingdom of God established.

When we find out who we are in Christ, our mind changes. We begin to understand the promises spoken to us about those who believe. So, when we believe, we come *into* what we believe. For example, once you believe in Christ Jesus, then you become "in Christ." And once you're in Christ, a whole new arena opens up for you, a complete new understanding, an entirely new attitude comes to your mind.

Chapter 4 — The Holy Spirit's Part in the Plan

The world contains many different cultures, including many nationalities, traditions, mindsets, and lifestyles. But the kingdom of God just reveals one culture. It's the culture of the King, and we are His sons and daughters.

I was born and raised in Oklahoma, where I accepted Christ as my Lord and Savior. So, I naturally tried to filter everything God spoke to me by the Spirit through my Oklahoma culture. But then I realized "old things have passed away." And, because they have, I'm no longer limited to that culture and attitude. I'm called to be a new creation. And I've been transferred out of the kingdom of darkness into the kingdom of light. So, now I no

longer reveal this world's culture. I'm of His
kingdom culture.

When we receive Jesus as our savior, our destiny
makes us become part of the age that is coming.
Remember we are seated with Him in heavenly
places. Even though we're living in this present age,
we belong to the age that is coming. So, as we
behold Him, we become more like Him. And the
more we become like Him in this present age, the
fullness of the age that is coming is released in this
age through us.

That's the kingdom!

The more we encounter the Lord, the more God
reveals Himself to us in Christ. And, the more the
age to come is shown to us in this age, the more it is
released through us. Therefore, in this age, the

people might know and taste of the age that is coming.

You might say that we are secret agents. We move through the cultures of earth as agents of the Better Country of the Kingdom of God. That is part of our purpose on the earth, to be His ambassadors, reconciling people to Him. It is in Christ that we live and move and have our being. Our life is hidden in Christ.

Let's return to our passage in Ephesians 1:

"Long before we first heard of Christ and got our hopes up, he had his eye on us, had designs on us for glorious living, part of the overall purpose he is working out in everything and everyone. It's in Christ that you, once you heard the truth and believed it (this message of your salvation), found yourself home free—signed, sealed, and delivered by the Holy Spirit. This signet from God is the first installment on what's coming, a reminder that we'll get everything God has planned for us, a praising and glorious life." vs. 11 - 14

God, the Father, has given us faith; he's given us Jesus; he's given us the Holy Spirit. The Holy Spirit is a down payment of things to come. The Holy Spirit is a friend. It's so vital for us to be baptized in the Holy Spirit. Jesus even commanded the disciples saying, "Don't go do anything until you receive the promise of the Father." And the promise of the Father is the Holy Spirit.

And when we get baptized in the Holy Spirit, He—the Holy Spirit—comes and lives within us. And His job is to reveal the things the Father has for us, to convict of sin, to intercede for us, and to help us in our weakness. John 16:5-15

That's why the devil doesn't want you to be baptized in the Holy Spirit. He doesn't want you to come into the fullness of who you are in Christ; he doesn't want you to understand the fullness of what God has for you.

But, God thought of everything. He gave you faith. He gave you Jesus. He gave you the Holy Spirit so you could walk through this age as an ambassador of all that is coming. Because of His equipping of us, we can be ambassadors of the realm that makes the lame walk, that opens blind eyes, that opens deaf

Being filled with the Holy Spirit is part of
his plan for you. To walk as his children
on the earth as his ambassadors, you
have to receive the Holy Spirit

ears. The works Jesus did? You're going to do yet
greater works. Why? Because the Father is living in
you, working through you to accomplish it for you.
Amen!

Being filled with the Holy Spirit is part of His plan
for you. In order to walk as His children on the earth
as His ambassadors, you must receive the Holy
Spirit. You can't even understand the things of the
Spirit of God without Him. We need the Holy Spirit
to give us revelation of the heart of God because
God is Spirit and those who worship Him must
worship Him in spirit and in truth. Without the Holy
Spirit, we can't even comprehend the things God

speaks to us by revelation because our carnal minds can't understand the things of the Spirit.

That's why we need to be baptized in the Holy Spirit.

Chapter 5 — To Live in His Perfect Plan

Now, that you know God has a perfect plan for you, how do you live in it?

The Bible tells us that "the Word became flesh" and "Jesus was the Word of God on the earth." So when I read the Scripture, I take it as a word that God is speaking to me. For example, when I read one of my favorite passages, Isaiah 41:8-13, in *The Message*, I put my name in it. Here is how I read it. And, you can too; just put your name in there.

"But you, [Doug,] my servant. You're [Doug,] my first choice, [a] descendant of my good friend Abraham. I pulled you in from the world, called you [Doug] in from every dark corner of the earth. I'm telling you [Doug,] you're my servant, serving on my side. I picked you, [Doug]. I haven't dropped you, [Doug]. Don't panic. I'm with you, [Doug]. There's no need for you to fear for I am your God, [Doug,] and I'll give you strength. I'll help you. I will hold you steady, keep a firm grip on you.

"Count on it, [Doug]. Everyone who had it in for you will end up out in the cold—real losers. Those who worked against you will end up empty handed—nothing to show for in their lives. When you go out looking for your old adversaries, you won't find them; not a trace of your old enemies, not even a memory. That's right, [Doug,] because I, your God, have a firm grip on you, and I'm not letting you go. I'm telling you, [Doug,] don't panic. I'm right here to help you."

That's so encouraging to me; I hope it is to you. Just realize that when our old adversaries and old lifestyles try to come back, we don't have to worry about it because old things have passed away. I can live out the Father's plan for my life because the old adversaries and the old plans of the enemy will no longer succeed in my life. Why? Because of His perfect plan for us. And it's perfect because of what the Father, Son, and Holy Spirit did and still do for us. They continue to work on our behalf to make His perfect plan succeed in your life and in mine.

And, this is the plan the Father has for each and every one of us: That we would come into an understanding of who we are in Christ, and that we understand the authority we have as sons in the Father's kingdom to walk on the earth. Even more than that, we can *do* the things the Father has predestined us to do in Christ Jesus and to reveal the love of the Father through Jesus Christ to the world.

I hope this book helps you explore His great plans for you and for all of us. I hope you've learned that

God is a Father and we are the focus of His love. And, because of that, we're being made holy and complete in His love.

Second, I hope you've learned that He adopted us into His family. He wants us to be children of His family. He wants to give us gifts and great blessings through Jesus Christ. Everything God has for us is found in Jesus.

And He wants us to know that He has set us free from our old lifestyle. Sin is no longer our master. We are no longer obligated to sin and our old lifestyles; we're new creatures. Old things have passed away, new things have come. We are now the righteousness of God in Christ; we are holy, complete, and lacking nothing. The Father wants us to know who we are in Christ Jesus.

He wants us to take ownership of the grace given to us. Remember, "...to each one of us grace was

Righteousness, peace, and joy are the byproducts of walking in the purpose of God and within the authority of His kingdom on the earth. The peace that passes understanding—that only Christ can give—will be ours.

given according to the measure of Christ's gift." (Ephesians 4:7, NASB). The Lord has called us to take responsibility for the administration of all the things He has given to us in Christ.

The Scripture says when we seek first His kingdom, all these things will be added to us. That means when we seek His rule and sovereignty in our lives, then grace will enable us to do what the Father has predestined us to do in Christ; in those things, we'll take on a heart of a servant. And then we will walk

29

in righteousness, peace, and joy. We will walk in the Holy Spirit. Then, we will truly live out His plan. And, then, our lives will reveal the fruits of His kingdom.

Righteousness, peace, and joy are the byproducts of walking in the purpose of God and within the authority of His kingdom on the earth. The peace that passes understanding—that only Christ can give—will be ours. Therefore, what weapon formed against us can prosper? What plan set against us can succeed?

When we come to the place of knowing that the Father has a plan for us and then understanding that plan, and knowing that the plan is found in Jesus, then it changes our whole attitude of who we are and what we have to do. And it releases us to walk in freedom. Where the Spirit of the Lord is, there is freedom, there is liberty. So it's no longer a task that we have to do, it is a joy set before us with authority given to us to accomplish His purpose He predestined for us.

So, Father, I thank you that you have a perfect plan. And, that You equip us to live that plan. As Isaiah told us, "You have worked wonders, Plans formed long ago, with perfect faithfulness." (Isaiah 25:1, NASB). You have called us, chosen us, and predestined us.

And Father, I pray that people that are reading this booklet will begin to hunger and seek after that which you have for them. And it's only found in Jesus. And when they find their place and their identity in Jesus, that the Holy Spirit will reveal the plans and the purpose that the Father has predestined for them and it will change and transform their life into a new understanding of who they are and what you've called them to be today on the earth.

In Jesus' name, Amen.

Group Discussion Guide

In order to allow the message of this book to penetrate the soil of your mind and heart, Doug and those who stand close to him in these things have prepared this guide of questions and discussion issues to help you work these truths into your life.

1. Why is it so important to know God as our Father?

2. Why does God choose to do His work through us?

3. Doug said that God has more faith in us than we have in God. How is that possible?

4. Do you believe that when God looks at you, He does not see who you *were*, only who you *are*?

5. Doug said, "It's one thing to go, but another thing to be sent." What does that mean to you?

6. Does this book help you to rise above the enemy's lies? Does it give you a higher view of God's love and plans for you?

7. The Bible says the Kingdom of God is within you. How does that happen?

8. Can you describe the culture of the Kingdom of God?

9. Have you been baptized in the Spirit? How has He made a difference in your life?

10. What does it mean that you can walk through the earth as an ambassador of the age to come?

11. How can we do "greater works" than Jesus when He was on earth?

12. Can your old enemies still harm you?

13. Do you understand the authority that the Father gives you?

14. Describe what this means to you: "Old things have passed away. New things have come."

www.ingramcontent.com/pod-product-compliance
Lightning Source LLC
Chambersburg PA
CBHW020444030426
42337CB00014B/1389